Y0-CSA-402

HOUGHTON MIFFLIN
Reading
A Legacy of Literacy

Special
Friends

HOUGHTON MIFFLIN   BOSTON • MORRIS PLAINS, NJ

California   •   Colorado   •   Georgia   •   Illinois   •   New Jersey   •   Texas

Design, Art Management, and Page Production: Studio Goodwin Sturges

Contents

Fussy Gail

by Anne Myers

illustrated by Kristina Stephenson

"Mama, can Gail eat lunch with us?" asked Little Bear.
"She can if she knocks this time!" smiled Mama Bear.

"It's Gail!" cried shy Little
Bear.

"What food do you like, Gail?"
asked Mama Bear.

"Food that isn't yucky," said
fussy Gail.

"Do you like chips?" asked
Mama Bear.

"They're too crunchy!"
groaned Gail.

"Do you like peanut butter
and jelly?" asked Mama Bear.
"It's too sticky," moaned
fussy Gail.

"Do you like wheat toast?"
asked Mama Bear.

"It's too dry," pouted Gail.

"Well!" said Mama Bear with a
sly smile. "I'll bet I can make
food that you will like."

"This is it," boasted Mama Bear.

"It's YUMMY!" sighed fussy Gail.

And she ate it up.

Sunny's Buddy

by Elena Vyadro
illustrated by Bob Kolar

Sunny felt lucky. He had a nice home on an ocean beach.

Sometimes Sunny felt sad, though. He needed some friends.

So Sunny wrote:
    Sunny's Open House
    Talk! Dance! Play Games!

Sunny cleaned his home. He
made jelly treats and fizzy
drinks. Sunny's home soon
filled up with friends.

Sunny's new friends played
games. They ate jelly treats,
drank fizzy drinks, and got dizzy
dancing.

What a nutty, silly bunch! Then
everyone went home.

Sunny looked around at his
messy home.

"My, my, my," moaned Sunny.
"Will I ever see my new friends
again?"

Sunny felt like he could cry.

Just then the doorbell rang. It
was Kitty from last night.

"I'll help you clean up, Sunny,"
smiled Kitty.

"Now that's a true buddy!"
claimed Sunny. He felt lucky.

I Spy

by Lynda Lazar
illustrated by Esther Szegedy

"That was a fun trip in the
city," said Miss Bly. "Let's
play 'I Spy' now."

"I spy Clyde's brand new penny," stated Molly.

"I spy Jeff's yummy candy," stated Holly.

"I spy Lyle's fluffy bunny," stated Polly.

"I spy blue sky," shouted Eddy.

"I spy wet ocean," shouted Teddy.

"I spy a sandy beach," shouted Freddy.

"I spy a fuzzy fly," yelled Sandy.

"I spy a dusty truck," yelled Andy.

"I spy muddy footprints," yelled Randy.

"I spy my shy puppy,"
squealed Netty.

"What else can you spy?"
asked Betty.

"I spy my mom and dad,"
squealed Netty.

"I spy my house," bragged
Jenny.

"I spy my buddy Kyle,"
bragged Lenny.

"I spy that sunny playground,"
bragged Kenny.

"I spy jolly kids," smiled Miss Bly, "going home. Good night!"

Bo's Bunnies

by Anne Myers
illustrated by Marsha Winborn

Bo has come to help Mother
Bunny with her bunnies.

"Just give them baths, hot
milk, and a nap," Mother Bunny
tells him.

Danny reaches for the soap
and bites it. Then he brushes
his teeth with it.

Frank splashes Missy. She is
unhappy and cries.

Bo shouts, "Don't be unkind, Frank."

Then he dries and dresses Missy.

Next, Bo fixes hot milk. Missy tosses cups into the pet dishes. Bo cleans the cups and refills them.

Bo reads and rereads *Big
Wishes*. Now the bunnies
are playing with Bo's glasses.
Bo's glasses land in the fish
tank. Bo fishes them out.

Then Bo takes the bunnies
outside and puts them in the
buggy. The three bunnies are
sleeping at last. So is Bo!

The Fleet Street Club

by Jordan Morris
illustrated by True Kelley

The Fleet Street kids wanted
a new clubhouse. So the kids
listed after-school jobs.

1. Bake cookies and cakes and sell them.
2. Wash cars.
3. Walk dogs and puppies.

4. Unload shopping bags.

5. Unpack boxes.

6. Trim shrubs.

Then the Fleet Street kids
made an ad. That next day, six
people asked for car washes
and dog walking.

Things went well, but then Fleet
Street's dog-walking team met
Fleet Street's car-washing team.
Six puppies ran with brushes
and made big splashes!

That day cars and dogs got
clean. Dogs got so clean that
six people asked for dog baths!

Soon that Fleet Street Club
had too many dogs, and
renamed itself the Fleet Street
Dog-Washing Club!

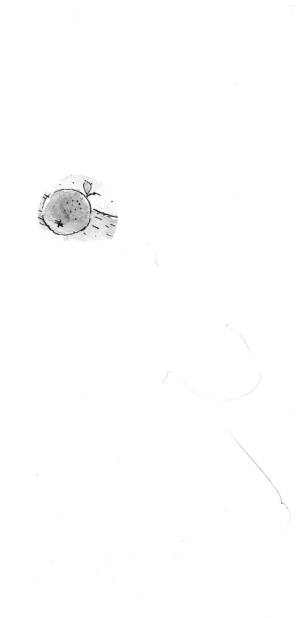

Peaches, Screeches

by Anne Myers
illustrated by Valeri Gorbachev

Fred Fox teaches cooking
classes.

"Wash up before cooking,"
Fred tells his class.

Fred unwraps some berries.
He mashes them up to make
milkshakes.

"Rewrap berries to keep them
fresh," Fred tells his class.

Next, Fred mixes up a cookie
mix and spoons it on a buttered
pan.

"Cookies will stick to an
ungreased pan," Fred tells his
class.

"For my last dish, I will make
Peaches, *Screeches*," Fred tells
his class. "Stack the peaches so
they stand 99 inches high."

The foxes are stacking peaches.
"Keep stacking," cries Fred.
"Stack them ten feet high!"
The foxes stack and restack.

The peach pile is as high as
Fred's hat.

"Keep stacking," repeats Fred.

Peaches are falling off the pile!
The foxes screech. Peaches land
everywhere!

"Well done!" crows Fred as he blows kisses to the foxes. "Now you know why I named my dish *Peaches, Screeches*!"

Jenny's Big Voice

by Malik Junot
illustrated by Dennis Hockerman

Jenny was big and graceful, but she had one big fault. When Jenny talked, she made lots of noise.

When Jenny spoke, rooms
shook. Others hid when
Jenny opened her mouth.
Jenny yawned loudly, too!

"Speak softly, Jenny," her
mom pleaded.

"Use an indoor voice, Jenny,"
her teacher begged.

"Nobody likes me!" bawled
Jenny.

One day Jenny had a painful
scratchy throat. She could not
speak! It was so peaceful at
Jenny's house that you could
hear a coin drop.

Jenny's mom wrapped Jenny
in a wool shawl and gave her
bowlfuls of hot soup. Jenny's
dad spoiled Jenny with
fancy toys.

Jenny's friends liked hearing
Jenny talk softly.

"Boy," Jenny claimed wisely,
"people like soft voices best."

Jenny got well, and she spoke like everyone else. Now and then, Jenny's big, big voice still came in handy.

Joy Boy

by Jordan Morris
illustrated by Anna Rich

One day Paul saw a stray dog.
His claw was stuck on a rusty
gate. The dog had cut his paw
on a sharp edge.

Paul took him home.
"Paul," Mom stated loudly,
"that dog can only stay a few
days. We have enough pets!"

Paul's dog was happy, so Paul
named him Joy Boy. Paul and
Joy Boy quickly became buddies.
They watched TV together at
night, too.

Paul showed Joy Boy tricks
and gave him handfuls of
crunchy treats. Sometimes Joy
Boy ate foil, too!

Joy Boy did helpful things.
When rabbits dug up the soil in
Mom's garden, Joy Boy chased
them over the lawn.

Joy Boy fetched toys for the
baby, too. Paul was hopeful
that Mom would let Joy Boy stay.

Joy Boy hauled newspapers
out of huge snow banks.

"Joy Boy," Mom cried at last,
"you're useful. You can stay!"

Shawn's Soy Sauce

by Anne Myers
illustrated by Pedro Martin

Shawn loved soy sauce. At dawn, Shawn had spoonfuls of soy sauce on his pancakes.

For lunch, Shawn had boiled
eggs with soy sauce and cupfuls
of raw beets with soy sauce.
At night, Shawn had broiled
fish with soy sauce.

When Shawn went out with friends, he would ask for ice cream. Then Shawn would pause.

"With soy sauce," he'd add.

One day, Shawn's town ran out of soy sauce. There just weren't enough people eating it, so the soy sauce plant closed.

Shawn had just one choice. He had to make his own soy sauce!

Shawn gladly grew a soybean garden. He watched his beans like a hawk. At night, Shawn put straw on the soil to keep his beans safe.

Shawn made soy sauce and kept it in a vault where it would not spoil. Now Shawn's zesty sauce is still there, for everyone to taste.

Word Lists

Theme 9, Week 1

Fussy Gail (p. 5) accompanies *When I Am Old with You.*

Decodable Words

New
<u>Sounds for y</u>: *crunchy, dry, fussy, jelly, shy, sly, sticky, yucky, yummy*

Previously Taught
and, asked, ate, bet, boasted, can, chips, cried, eat, food, Gail, groaned, if, is, isn't, it, it's, knocks, like, lunch, make, Mama, moaned, peanut, pouted, she, sighed, smile, smiled, that, this, time, toast, too, up, us, well, wheat, will, with, you

High-Frequency Words

Previously Taught
a, Bear, butter, do, I, I'll, Little, said, they're, what

Theme 9, Week 1

Sunny's Buddy (p. 13) accompanies *When I Am Old with You.*

Decodable Words

New
<u>Sounds for y</u>: *buddy, cry, dizzy, fizzy, jelly, Kitty, lucky, messy, my, nutty, silly, Sunny, Sunny's*

Previously Taught
an, and, at, ate, beach, bunch, claimed, clean, cleaned, drank, drinks, felt, filled, from, games, got, had, he, help, his, home, house, it, just, last, like, looked, made, moaned, needed, new, nice, night, now, on, play, played, rang, sad, see, smiled, so, soon, that's, then, treats, true, up, went, will, with, wrote, you

High-Frequency Words

New
around, dance, dancing, ever, ocean, open, talk, though

Previously Taught
a, again, could, doorbell, everyone, friends, I, I'll, some, sometimes, the, they, was, what

Theme 9, Week 1

I Spy (p. 21) accompanies *When I Am Old with You.*

Decodable Words

New
Sounds for *y*: Andy, Betty, Bly, buddy, bunny, candy, city, Clyde's, dusty, Eddy, fluffy, fly, Freddy, fuzzy, Holly, Jenny, jolly, Kenny, Kyle, Lenny, Lyle's, Molly, muddy, my, Netty, penny, Polly, puppy, Randy, sandy, Sandy, shy, sky, spy, sunny, Teddy, yummy

Previously Taught
and, asked, beach, blue, bragged, brand, can, dad, footprints, fun, going, good, home, house, in, Jeff's, kids, let's, Miss, mom, new, night, now, play, playground, shouted, smiled, squealed, stated, that, trip, truck, wet, yelled, you

High-Frequency Words

New
else, ocean

Previously Taught
a, I, said, the, was, what

Theme 9, Week 2

Bo's Bunnies (p. 29) accompanies *The New Friend.*

Decodable Words

New
Base Words and Endings -es, -ies: brushes, dishes, dresses, fishes, fixes, glasses, reaches, splashes, tosses, wishes, bunnies, cries, dries

Prefixes *re-, un-:* refills, rereads, unhappy, unkind

Previously Taught
and, at, baths, be, big, bites, Bo, Bo's, buggy, Bunny, cleans, cups, Danny, fish, Frank, has, he, help, him, his, hot, in, is, it, just, land, last, milk, Missy, nap, next, now, out, outside, pet, playing, reads, she, shouts, sleeping, so, soap, takes, tank, teeth, tells, them, then, three, with

(Bo's Bunnies, continued)

High-Frequency Words

Previously Taught
a, are, come, don't, for, give, her, into, Mother, puts, the, to

Theme 9, Week 2

The Fleet Street Club (p. 37) accompanies The New Friend.

Decodable Words

New
Base Words and Endings -es, -ies: boxes, brushes, splashes, washes, cookies, puppies

Prefixes re-, un-: renamed, unload, unpack

Previously Taught
ad, an, and, asked, bags, bake, baths, big, but, cakes, clean, Club, clubhouse, day, dog, dogs, Fleet, got, had, itself, jobs, kids, listed, made, met, new, next, ran, sell, shopping, shrubs, six, so, soon, Street, Street's, team, that, them, then, things, too, trim, well, went, with

High-Frequency Words

New
after-school, car-washing, dog-washing, wash, washes

Previously Taught
a, car, cars, dog-walking, for, many, people, the, walk, walking, wanted

Theme 9, Week 2

Peaches, Screeches (p. 45) accompanies The New Friend.

Decodable Words

New
Base Words and Endings -es, -ies: classes, foxes, inches, kisses, mashes, mixes, peaches, screeches, teaches, berries, cookies, cries

Prefixes re-, un-: restack, repeats, rewrap, ungreased, unwraps

Previously Taught
an, and, as, blows, but, class, cookie, cooking, crows, dish, feet, Fox, Fred, Fred's, fresh, hat, he, high, his, is, it, keep, know, land, last, make, milkshakes, mix, my, named, next, now, on, pan, peach, pile,

78

(*Peaches, Screeches,* Previously Taught Decodable Words continued)
screech, so, spoons, stack, stacking, stand, stick, tells, ten, them, up, well, why, will, you

High-Frequency Words
New
before, done, off, wash

Previously Taught
a, are, buttered, everywhere, falling, for, I, some, the, they, to

Theme 9, Week 3
Jenny's Big Voice (p. 53) accompanies *The Surprise Family.*

Decodable Words
New
Vowel Pairs *oi, oy, au, aw: coin, noise, spoiled, voice, voices, boy, toys, fault, bawled, shawl, yawned*

Suffixes *-ful, -ly, -y: bowlfuls, graceful, painful, peaceful, loudly, softly, wisely, handy, scratchy*

Previously Taught
an, and, at, begged, best, big, but, came, claimed, dad, day, drop, fancy, gave, got, had, hid, hot, house, in, it, Jenny, Jenny's, like, liked, likes, lots, made, me, mom, mouth, not, now, pleaded, rooms, she, shook, so, soft, soup, speak, spoke, still, that, then, throat, too, use, well, when, with, wool, wrapped, you

High-Frequency Words
Previously Taught
a, could, else, everyone, friends, hear, hearing, her, indoor, nobody, of, one, opened, others, people, talk, talked, teacher, was

Theme 9, Week 3
Joy Boy (p. 61) accompanies *The Surprise Family.*

Decodable Words
New
Vowel Pairs *oi, oy, au, aw: foil, soil, Boy, Joy, toys, hauled, Paul, Paul's, claw, lawn, paw, saw*

(*Joy Boy*, New Decodable Words continued)

Suffixes -ful, -ly, -y: handfuls, helpful, hopeful, useful, loudly, quickly, crunchy, rusty

Previously Taught
and, at, ate, banks, became, buddies, can, chased, cried, cut, day, days, did, dog, dug, fetched, few, gate, gave, had, happy, him, his, home, huge, in, last, let, Mom, Mom's, named, night, on, out, pets, rabbit's, showed, snow, so, stated, stay, stray, stuck, that, them, things, too, took, treats, tricks, TV, up, we, when, you

High-Frequency Words

New
baby, edge, enough, garden, only, sharp, together, watched

Previously Taught
a, for, have, newspapers, of, one, over, sometimes, the, they, was, would, you're

Theme 9, Week 3

Shawn's Soy Sauce (p. 69) accompanies *The Surprise Family*.

Decodable Words

New
Vowel Pairs oi, oy, au, aw: boiled, broiled, choice, soil, spoil, soy, pause, sauce, vault, dawn, hawk, raw, Shawn, Shawn's, straw
Suffixes -ful, -ly, -y: cupfuls, spoonfuls, gladly, zesty

Previously Taught
add, and, ask, at, beans, beets, closed, cream, day, eating, eggs, fish, grew, had, he, he'd, his, ice, in, is, it, just, keep, kept, like, lunch, made, make, night, not, now, on, out, own, pancakes, plant, ran, safe, so, soybean, still, taste, then, town, went, when, with

High-Frequency Words

New
garden, enough, watched

Previously Taught
a, everyone, for, friends, loved, of, one, people, put, the, there, to, weren't, where, would